A Note from PJ Library®

Marc Chagall, the famous Jewish painter (1887-1985), is one of the most important artists of the twentieth century. When Chagall rose to prominence, few Jewish artists had achieved his fame and influence; even fewer had done so painting overtly Jewish imagery. Born Moishe Segal, Chagall left his home in Belarus to study and make art in big cities like St. Petersburg and Paris. But no matter where he went, his heritage followed him, and unlike some other Jewish artists, Chagall let his artwork reflect that.

Many of Chagall's most well-known works feature Jewish scenes, such as "The Canopy," which portrays a couple getting married beneath a *chuppah* (wedding canopy), or "The Praying Jew," featuring a man wearing a *tallit* (prayer shawl). But as Chagall's fame attests, his appeal stretches beyond the Jewish community. He is remembered not only as a major Jewish artist but also one of the major modernists. "If a painter is Jewish and paints life," he once said, "how can he help having Jewish elements in his work? But if he is a good painter, there will be more than that. The Jewish element will be there, but the art will tend to approach the universal." The art world – and the Jewish world – is richer for it. To learn more, visit pjlibary.org/apictureformarc.

PJ Library®

JEWISH BEDTIME STORIES and SONGS

A Note from PJ Library®

One of Chagall's famous paintings, "The Fiddler, " is shown on the back of this book. This evocative 1913 painting was part of the inspiration for the 1964 Broadway musical *Fiddler on the Roof*, which depicts life in a Jewish *shtetl* (Yiddish for "little town") very similar to Chagall's hometown, Vitebsk.

✡ Can you find the place in the book where Marc describes some elements of this painting?

✡ Chagall once described himself as "a dreamer who never woke up." What's dreamlike about this painting?

✡ Search the web for other Chagall paintings. Be on the lookout for flying, dreamlike scenes, and elements that represent life in Vitebsk.

✡ Try making some of your own Chagall-style art. Which scenes from your life would you include?

About PJ Library

The gift of PJ Library is made possible by many generous supporters, your local Jewish community, and the Harold Grinspoon Foundation. PJ Library shares Jewish culture and values through quality children's books that reflect the diversity of Jewish customs and practice. To learn more about the program, and ways to connect to activities in your area, visit pjlibrary.org.

A Picture for Marc

by **Eric A. Kimmel**
illustrated by **Matthew Trueman**

A STEPPING STONE BOOK™
Random House 🏠 New York

For Colleen—E.A.K.

For Daniel and Ellie—M.T.

Text copyright © 2007 by Eric A. Kimmel
Illustrations copyright © 2007 by Matthew Trueman

Published in the United States by Random House Children's Books,
a division of Random House, Inc., New York. Originally published in
hardcover by Random House, Inc., in 2007. First paperback edition 2008.

Random House and colophon are registered trademarks and A Stepping
Stone Book and colophon are trademarks of Random House, Inc.

Visit us on the Web!
www.steppingstonesbooks.com
www.randomhouse.com/kids

Educators and librarians, for a variety of teaching tools, visit us at
www.randomhouse.com/teachers

The Library of Congress has cataloged the hardcover edition of this work
as follows:
Kimmel, Eric A.
A picture for Marc / by Eric A. Kimmel ; illustrated by Matthew Trueman.
   p.   cm. — ("Stepping Stone book.")
Summary: Marc, an imaginative Russian boy, discovers his talent for drawing
and, with the encouragement of a friend and an art teacher, decides to become
an artist. Based loosely on the childhood of Marc Chagall.
ISBN 978-0-375-83253-6 (jacketed hardcover) —
ISBN 978-0-375-93253-3 (lib. bdg.) — ISBN 978-0-375-85225-1 (pbk.)
1. Chagall, Marc, 1887–1985—Juvenile fiction. [1. Chagall, Marc, 1887–1985—
Fiction. 2. Artists—Fiction.] I. Trueman, Matthew, ill. II. Title.
PZ7.K5648Pic 2007   [Fic]—dc22   2006029617

Printed in the United States of America
10 9 8 7 6 5 4 3 2 1

061829.5K1/B1213/A8

Contents

1. The Dullest Town in the World   1

2. Finding a Picture   10

3. A Fiddler on the Roof   20

4. A Real Artist   30

5. A World of Pictures   39

6. Pitchkas!   53

7. The Herring Artist   64

8. Over Vitebsk   88

Author's Note   99

1

The Dullest Town in the World

*T*he sign in the railway station read:

WELCOME TO VITEBSK

Some people thought it should also say:

(THE DULLEST TOWN IN THE WORLD)

Of all the towns in Russia, Vitebsk had to be the dullest. The place was hundreds of years old, but nobody could remember anything important ever happening there.

There was nothing to see. No mountains.

No beautiful lakes or streams. Swamps and fields surrounded Vitebsk. A sluggish river flowed through the center of town.

Vitebsk had a town museum, but nobody went there. The museum contained only a walnut that looked like a man's head, a postcard from Spain, a portrait of a knight whose name nobody could remember, and a rusty sword that someone found in a field. It was the dullest museum in the world.

Every once in a while, a tourist would get off the train, look around, and get back on again. Nobody wanted to stay in such a boring town. Even the people who lived in Vitebsk knew it was dull. They had no idea why they lived there, except that it was too much trouble to move.

Not one famous person had ever visited Vitebsk. Not one important person had ever lived in Vitebsk. Not one noteworthy person had ever been born in Vitebsk, the dullest town in the world.

One boy, however, did not think Vitebsk was dull at all. Marc Chagall looked at the world through different eyes. Where others saw a dull, ordinary town, he saw a place filled with magic. Every moment was a wonder.

A rooster with a bright red comb crowing on a fence.

A flock of snow white geese walking through muddy streets on their way to the market.

An old chestnut horse pulling a wagon.

A gray-bearded fiddler playing his violin.

The daily life in the street, in the house, on the rooftops never seemed dull to Marc. There were so many exciting things happening every day. The problem was that nobody else ever noticed them. Marc tried and tried, but he could not make others see what he saw.

"Look at that chicken!" he said to his father when they went to the market. "Look at all the shadings in her feathers! Isn't it amazing how they catch the sunlight!"

"Yes," Marc's father said. "It's a chicken. Chickens have feathers. So what?"

Another time, Marc and his sister went for a walk in the fields outside the town. They stopped to rest beside the road. Marc leaned back and looked up at the sky.

"Did you ever look at the clouds?" he asked his sister.

"Why should I?" she answered. "Clouds are clouds."

"No, they're not!" said Marc. "No two clouds are ever the same. You have to look at them. Really look hard. Each one is different. Can you see how the clouds change as they float along? They rise and swell like the dough in the bowl when Mama makes bread on Friday. Close your eyes and count to a hundred. When you open them again, you'll see a whole sky of new clouds. Maybe God makes clouds the way Mama makes bread. What do you think?"

"I think you're crazy," said his sister. "Who cares what clouds do? Who cares who makes them? They're up in the sky and we're here on the ground. If you go around with your nose in the air, looking at clouds, you're going to tumble into a ditch and break your head. So there!"

"I think the brass buttons on your blue coat are beautiful," Marc once said to a policeman. "Did you know that they shine like disks of fire when they catch the sun?"

"What? Are you making fun of me?" said the policeman. "I'm going to put you in jail!"

Marc had to run, for fear that the policeman might do just that.

"Why is it so hard to make people see?" Marc asked his mother. He held the dustpan while she swept the floor.

"Maybe they don't want to see," Marc's

mother answered. "What good is this *seeing* you talk about? Will it put money in your pocket? Can it put food on the table or keep a roof over your head? Will it feed the hungry? Will it put new clothes on the poor people who go about in rags?"

She swept the dust into the dustpan. "What you call 'seeing,' I call 'wasting time.' It seems to me, Marc, that if you have time to look at clouds and chickens and buttons, then you have time to study your schoolbooks. If you want to look at something, why don't you go look at your homework?"

Marc emptied the dustpan. He went to the table and opened his schoolbooks. He stared at all the sentences he was supposed to copy and correct for his Russian lesson. Marc sighed. He began copying the first sentence when he noticed the cat. She was sleeping on a chair, looking like a great

round pillow of fur. Marc put down his pencil and watched the cat. He watched how
her breath went in and out, in and out, so
softly it seemed she wasn't breathing at all.

"Maybe people don't see things the way
I do," he said to himself. "What if I could
find a way to show them what I see, what I
feel, when I look at the cat?"

Marc was wondering about that an hour
later, when his mother came to check on
him. He was still looking at the cat. The
page in his notebook was empty. He had yet
to finish copying a single sentence.

"Marc, leave the cat alone! Stop day-
dreaming and do your homework!" his
mother shouted.

"Yes, Mother." Marc sighed as he began
to write down the words. The reason for
schoolwork was one thing Marc could never
see at all, no matter how hard he tried.

2

Finding a Picture

School was Marc's biggest problem. He could not find any wonder or excitement in it. He could find magic in a goat. He could find beauty in a wagon. He could find amazing shapes in an old horseshoe nailed to a stable door.

Marc tried and tried, but it was no use. School remained as dreary as the old books in the library. School was the dullest place in

Vitebsk, the dullest town in all of Russia.

This meant that Marc's school had to be the dullest, most boring place in the world.

Marc was not happy about feeling this way. He was not happy that his grades were poor. He didn't like getting bad marks for not completing his work or not handing it in on time. He knew how hard his parents had to work to send him to school. Marc was not supposed to be at this school at all.

Marc's school was a Russian school. Jewish boys like Marc were not allowed to go there. However, in Russia, there were ways of getting around even the strictest rules. Marc's mother bribed a teacher to let Marc into his class. It cost fifty rubles, a huge amount of money for a poor family.

Marc's mother thought it was worth it. She would have paid twice as much to make sure he got a good education. The *heder,* the

Jewish school, taught boys how to read Hebrew, say their prayers, and read the Torah. It did not teach science or mathematics. It did not teach history or geography. It did not even teach Russian, the country's national language. The only languages used in the *heder* were the two Jewish languages, Hebrew and Yiddish.

The *heder* was only for boys. Jewish girls did not go to school.

"Why is the world so unfair?" Marc asked himself. He knew his sisters wanted to go to school. They were all smart. They would have done well. But since they were girls, there was no hope that they would ever enter a classroom. School was not for girls. Not even the *heder*.

Marc, on the other hand, hated school and did poorly. Yet he was the one who got to go. Marc couldn't decide if his luck was good or bad. During history and Russian, his worst subjects, it seemed mostly bad. There was only one bright spot in his long, boring day. That was geometry class.

Their teacher, Professor Mirsky, taught the boys all about shapes. They studied circles, triangles, rectangles. They learned about spheres and cubes. They measured angles and lines.

Most important, they learned how to draw. Professor Mirsky showed them how to use a protractor and compass to make the exact shapes he drew on the blackboard. Marc was the best student in the class. He wished he could spend the whole day making triangles and squares. Professor Mirsky praised his work to the other students.

"All of you need to try harder," he said. "Marc is the only one who really knows how to draw."

Professor Mirsky wrote the assignment on the blackboard. The class got to work. Marc completed it quickly. He raised his hand, but Professor Mirsky was explaining a problem to another student and did not see him. Marc put his hand down and thought about what to do next. The rest of the class was still working.

Marc glanced at Victor, the boy across the aisle. Victor was writing in his notebook. Marc wondered what was taking him so long. The assignment was not hard and Victor was usually among the first ones finished.

Marc leaned across the aisle to see what Victor was doing. He was drawing a picture! Marc was amazed. He had never seen anyone draw a picture before. He did not know it could be done.

"What is that? What are you doing?" Marc was so excited. He struggled to keep his voice to a whisper.

Victor looked up. "I'm making a picture. Drawing shapes gets boring. This is more fun." He held up his picture for Marc to see. He had drawn a gentleman with long whiskers and rows of medals on the front of his uniform.

"How do you do that?" Marc asked.

"It's easy. You don't have to be smart. It doesn't take any special talent," Victor said. "Watch. I'll show you how." Victor showed Marc how he placed a blank piece of paper over a picture in a magazine and traced it.

"You go to the library and look through the magazines," Victor explained. "When you find a picture you like, check out the magazine and trace the image. That's how you make your own picture."

"Is that all? I could do that!" Marc exclaimed.

"Of course you can," said Victor. "Draw-ing isn't hard. It just takes practice."

Marc couldn't wait until school was over. He hurried to the public library. "I'm look-ing for a magazine," he told the librarian.

"What kind of magazine?" the librarian asked.

"One with pictures," said Marc.

The librarian frowned. "What sort of pic-tures did you have in mind?"

"Just pictures," Marc replied.

The librarian brought Marc several copies of a magazine called *Niva*. Pictures filled the pages. "Look through these. Perhaps you'll find what you want."

Marc took the magazines to a table. He turned through the pages one by one. He glanced at many pictures, but none seemed like ones he'd want to draw.

Marc saw plenty of pictures like the one Victor was drawing: uniformed men with lots of whiskers and lots of medals. There were pictures of railroads and palaces. There was a picture of a huge turnip and another of a group of hunters standing around a dead tiger. Marc had never seen a live tiger, but the sight of such a beautiful animal lying dead on the ground made him feel sad. He didn't want to draw a picture like that. He turned the page.

Now here was something interesting! This magazine had a story about Anton Rubinstein, the musical genius. He was one of the most famous musicians in Russia. And he was born into a Jewish family, too!

If Anton Rubinstein could be a success, so could Marc Chagall! Marc knew at once that this was the picture he wanted to draw. He took the magazine to the librarian.

"Did you find what you needed?" he asked.

"Yes," said Marc. "I want to read about Anton Rubinstein."

"An excellent choice," the librarian said. "Are you interested in music?"

"No, drawing," said Marc. The librarian gave him a peculiar look, but Marc didn't notice. By then, he was out the door and on his way home with the magazine tucked under his arm.

3

A Fiddler on the Roof

Marc sat at the kitchen table. He opened the magazine and stared at the picture. He had no idea how to begin.

"How does one draw a picture?" Marc asked himself. He tried to remember what Victor had showed him. Of course! He had traced it.

Marc placed a piece of paper over the picture of Anton Rubinstein. His pencil wandered along, tracing the faint lines of the magazine as they showed through the paper. It was like following a cow path through a meadow. The lines went here. The lines went there. Marc drew a lot of lines, but he couldn't see anything that looked like a picture.

"This can't be right," Marc said to himself. "I wonder if Victor is playing a trick on me. There must be more to drawing a picture than tracing lines."

Marc lifted the paper from the magazine and looked at it. There was a picture inside those lines. There had to be. How could he find it?

Just for fun, Marc connected two of the lines. He added some more lines of his own. An eye suddenly appeared on the paper, where before there had been only meaning-less scribbles.

"That's it!" he exclaimed. "I understand now." He kept drawing. Another eye appeared. They were Anton Rubinstein's eyes, small and surrounded by wrinkles.

Marc sat back in his chair. He trembled with excitement. The great composer's face filled the paper. Marc had drawn his crinkled features, the wrinkles across his brow, his shock of white hair. He seemed to be smiling at Marc. Marc imagined him saying, "This is very good for your first try. Keep working at it."

Marc looked at the picture he had drawn and compared it with the one in the magazine. They were different. Rubinstein was definitely not smiling in the magazine picture. He looked stern and severe, as if he were about to scold a member of the orchestra for hitting a wrong note.

"How can that be? They're the same

picture." Then Marc understood. "No, they're not. There's a difference between drawing and tracing. Drawing a picture has to be more than just copying. When I draw a picture, I put part of myself into it. That's what makes the picture come alive. I make it my own."

Marc stopped to think about this. He wondered if Victor had made this discovery, or if his friend was happy to trace pictures exactly as they were in the magazine.

"I'll do another," Marc said. He turned the pages, looking for another picture to draw. Here was one! It was a picture of a woman in Greece, holding a lamb.

This time Marc did not bother with tracing. He took a new sheet of paper and began to draw. He hardly had to look at the magazine at all. He knew what a lamb looked like. The woman from Greece was

not so different from the country women who came to the market in Vitebsk to sell vegetables, chickens, baskets, and cloth that they wove and embroidered themselves.

Marc drew what he knew from the town he lived in. When he was done, he compared his picture with the one in the magazine. Again, they were different. The woman in Marc's picture was a stout Russian woman, fair and blond, with a wide, happy face. The lamb squirmed in her arms, as if it couldn't wait to run off to a meadow.

Marc liked his second picture even more than the first. He looked through the magazine for a third picture to draw. He couldn't find one. None of the pictures seemed interesting to him.

Maybe I should bring this magazine back to the library and check out a different one, Marc thought. However, he didn't feel like walking all the way to the library. He wanted to draw something now.

Suddenly he had another idea. "Why do I need a magazine at all? I don't have to copy somebody else's picture. I can make my own."

Marc set the magazine aside. He took another blank piece of paper and let his pencil wander around like a chicken searching for bugs in the dirt. He put his pencil down and looked at what he had drawn. "That looks like an old man with a beard," Marc said to himself. He added more lines. "It's Grandfather!"

Marc laughed as he drew his grandfather, the butcher of Lyozno, the little town where his mother came from. Marc remembered a time when his grandfather disappeared. They looked all over town. No one could find him. Then they saw him. He had taken a sack of carrots and climbed up to the roof of his house to eat them. Marc drew his grandfather sitting on the roof.

And then he thought, *This looks more like Uncle Noah than Grandfather.* With a few lines, Marc turned Grandfather into Uncle Noah. Since Uncle Noah played the violin, Marc drew a fiddle for the man on the roof to play.

Marc smiled. He liked this picture. He still had a little space left in the corner, so he drew his grandfather tugging a calf on a rope. The sad-eyed calf hung his head, as if the poor animal knew what waited for him at the butcher shop. Marc could almost hear his grandfather saying, "Don't look at me that way. Who told you to be a calf? You should have been a bird." Marc drew a swallow flying above the rooftops.

The swallow made Marc think about the

village of Lyozno and how much he wished
he were there. "If I could fly, I'd go there
right now," said Marc. He drew a picture of
himself, flying with the swallow above the
village.

Marc studied his picture. He had never seen anything like it. "It reminds me of a dream," he said. "Maybe I can make my dreams come true with pictures." Marc put his drawing down and thought about what he had just learned.

"I don't have to copy a picture from a book or magazine. I don't have to draw things that are real. My pictures can be whatever I want them to be. There is no end to my pictures. They can be whatever I imagine, whatever I dream."

4

A Real Artist

"I have something to show you," Marc whispered to his friend Victor at school the next day. They were in geometry class again. Professor Mirsky stood at the blackboard, reviewing different types of triangles.

"What is it?" Victor asked.

Marc passed him an envelope. "Never mind. Just take a look and tell me what you think."

"Gentlemen?" Professor Mirsky asked. He looked toward the left side of the room, where Marc and Victor sat.

Victor slipped the envelope into his book bag. Marc began writing in his notebook.

Victor caught up with Marc after school. He handed back the envelope. "These are wonderful!" Victor said. "Where did you find these pictures? I've never seen anything like them. Tell me what magazine they came from. I want to copy them, too."

"I didn't copy these pictures," Marc explained. "I drew them myself."

"By yourself?" said Victor. "How can you do that?"

"I just began drawing," said Marc. "At first, I copied pictures from a magazine, the way you showed me. Then I thought, *Why bother making a picture that already exists?* I started changing the pictures in little ways.

I liked doing that. Then I thought, *Why not make my own?* So I did. I'm really glad you like my drawings. I didn't know if they were good or not."

"They're *very* good, Marc," Victor said. "As soon as I looked at them, I said to myself, 'Marc is an artist.'"

Marc had never heard the word *artist* before. "What's that?" he asked Victor.

Victor laughed. "Don't you know? How can you draw so well and not even know what an artist is? An artist is a person who makes pictures."

Marc shrugged. "If I'm an artist, so are you. You're the one who showed me how to make a picture."

"It's not the same," Victor said. "I showed you how to copy. Being an artist is more than that."

Marc still didn't understand. "What is it?"

Victor thought for a minute. "I know someone who can explain it better than I can! Come with me."

Marc followed Victor through twisting lanes and alleys. They came to a tiny street where Marc had never been. Small shops lined both sides of the street. Brightly painted signs in their windows told what each was selling.

Books, New & Used
Bread & Pastries
Paint & Hardware
Cheese, Milk & Eggs

The sign in the window of the last shop on the street read:

School of Painting & Drawing
Yehuda Pen, Artist

"He's an artist, that Mr. Pen. The sign says so," said Victor. "Go ask him. He'll know."

"I can't just knock on a stranger's door. I'm embarrassed. Come with me," said Marc.

"You don't need me to hold your hand," said Victor. "Just go knock on the door. Ask Mr. Pen the same question you asked me. If anyone in Vitebsk can tell you what an artist does, he'll be the one."

"What if he's busy? What if he gets angry with me for bothering him?" Marc began to wish he had never shown Victor his drawings.

"He won't get angry," Victor assured Marc. "Maybe he can teach you how to be a better artist. You won't know until you ask him."

"You're right," said Marc. He bent down in the street to tie his shoelaces. When he got up again, Victor was gone. Marc stood alone in the street, in front of the artist's shop. He knew he could just go home. No one would ever know what happened, not even Victor.

Or he could knock on the door. That is what Marc decided to do. "I want to know what an artist does," he said to himself. "Mr. Pen is the only one in Vitebsk who knows the answer. If I don't ask him, I may never find out."

Marc gathered his courage. However, before he could do anything, the door opened by itself. A short man with a trimmed, prickly beard looked out. "Are you waiting for someone, boy?" he asked.

"I want to talk to Mr. Pen," Marc answered.

"About what?" the man asked him.

"I want to find out about being an artist," Marc said. "What does an artist do?"

The man stroked his beard. "Do you know the story of Rabbi Hillel and the man from Greece?"

"Do you mean the one where the Greek man asked him to teach him the whole Torah while he stood on one foot?" said Marc. "Everybody knows that story. We learned it in *heder*. Rabbi Hillel told the man, 'If something is hateful to you, do not do it to others.'"

"That's the one. I am not as wise as Rabbi Hillel," the man said. "You have asked a deep and important question. I can't answer it with a few words while we stand in the street. You will have to come inside so we can have a talk."

"I don't mind," said Marc.

"Then please come in. What is your name?" the man asked.

"Me?" said Marc. "I'm Marc Chagall."

The man shook his hand. "And I am Yehuda Pen."

5

A World of Pictures

Marc followed Mr. Pen up the stairs to his studio. The sharp smell of fresh paint prickled his nose. They entered a room at the top of the landing. Marc looked around. It was as if he had crossed into another world. Faces stared at him from the four walls.

He had entered a world of pictures. They covered the walls. They stood propped up in corners. They lay stacked on the floor.

Several easels in the middle of the room held canvases with half-finished pictures. Brushes and tubes of paint were lined up beside them on small tables.

"Did you make all these?" Marc asked.

"Not all," Mr. Pen said. "Some are mine. Others were painted by my students. Some are by friends of mine, other artists whose work I admire. I like to think of these pictures as my children. As you can see, I have a big family. There is hardly enough room here for all of them."

Marc turned around slowly, staring at the pictures. "Is this what an artist does?" Marc asked. "Make pictures?"

"That's part of it," said Mr. Pen. "Not every artist makes pictures. Some artists work with metal, some with stone, some with wood, and some with clay. It doesn't matter what the artist works with. What is really important is what the artist sees."

"What do you mean?" asked Marc.

"I'll show you," Mr. Pen said. "Walk around the room. Find a picture that you like, or at least one that interests you. We'll talk about it."

Marc's eyes drifted up and down as he studied the paintings on the walls. He paused, then walked on. Finally, he stopped before a large portrait of three people. A bald man with a beard wore a uniform covered with medals. A tiny woman in a green velvet dress sat beside him. In between stood a little girl in a dark blue frock. She had a yellow ribbon in her hair.

Mr. Pen came over to where Marc was standing. "Is that the one you like?" he asked.

"No!" Marc exclaimed. "I don't like it at all."

"Ah! The picture makes you feel something. That's a good start," Mr. Pen said. "What are you thinking when you look at these people?"

"They're selfish and piggy," said Marc. "The man, especially. He has little eyes just like a pig. Look at the way his hand rests on the woman's chair. He seems to be saying, 'This chair is mine. This woman is mine. The little girl is mine. Everything you see in this picture is mine . . . mine . . . mine!'"

"Very good," said Mr. Pen. "And what about the woman?"

"That's his wife," said Marc. "She can't stand him, but she puts up with him because she is as greedy as he is. She likes living in a huge house with lots of servants. She likes riding around in a big carriage."

"What else?" Mr. Pen asked.

Mark stood in front of the little girl.

"This one is the worst of the three. She's completely spoiled. Nobody dares tell her not to do something because they're afraid she'll complain to her parents."

Marc stepped closer to the painting. He stared at the little girl's face. "All the same, I have to feel sorry for her. She isn't very happy. She has no friends and she'll never have any. She'll grow up to marry someone as awful as her father and have children as spoiled as she is."

"Can you tell all that from the picture?" Mr. Pen asked.

"Of course," said Marc. "It's all there. See how they stand and sit." He pointed to the people in the painting to show Mr. Pen what he meant.

"They're supposed to be a family, yet they're not even looking at each other," Marc went on. "They don't connect in any way. They could as easily be three strangers brought together by accident."

Mr. Pen nodded. "That's very good, Marc. Everything you've said is true. Of course, I don't believe that Baron Karpf or his family would be happy to hear those thoughts. Let's keep them between ourselves. The baron is extremely pleased with this painting. He and the baroness dropped by to see it yesterday. I am going to deliver it to their house later this week."

"How can they like seeing themselves that way?" Marc asked.

"It's because they don't see themselves that way at all," said Mr. Pen. "This painting will be hung in the grand ballroom of their house. They will be able to look at themselves every day and be reminded of how rich they are and how much they have. That's what they wanted and that's what I painted for them. What they don't understand is that a picture can also be a magic mirror. It can show what you want to see, if you don't care to look too deeply. But if you take the time to look—*really* look—it can show you much more. More, perhaps, than you want to know. But artists can't help that. They must paint what they see. Would you like to talk about another picture?"

"Yes," said Marc. "You pick one this time."

Mr. Pen walked around the room. He stopped in front of a painting hanging on the opposite wall, across from the picture of Baron Karpf and his family.

"How about this one?" Mr. Pen asked. "What do you see?"

Marc studied the picture. "I see a Jewish man. He has a short beard and side curls, with a cap on his head. He wears a long

brown coat with large buttons. He holds a
cane in his right hand and carries a basket
on his left arm. The basket is closed, but I
think I know what is inside it."

"What?" asked Mr. Pen.

"Pretzels," said Marc.

"What makes you think that?" Mr. Pen asked.

"Because I know this man," Marc said. "I see dozens like him in the market. The man is very poor. He lives from day to day. His wife bakes pretzels and he sells them in the marketplace. If he has a good day and sells his pretzels, he can afford to buy herring and black bread for his family's dinner. If not, they eat pretzels."

"Anything else? What do you see in his face? Tell me more about this man," Mr. Pen asked. "Why do you think I wanted to paint his picture? He certainly couldn't afford to pay me for it, like Baron Karpf."

Marc had to think about this question for a long time before he could answer. "He is just a poor man. He believes in God, but now he is beginning to wonder if God believes in him. He is getting older. He walks with a cane. What will happen to his family if he can no longer sell his pretzels? So many people depend on him. He is worried, but he has not given up. I think that is why you painted him. You saw the courage in his tired face."

"To an artist, the man who sells pretzels in the street can be as important as the governor of a province," said Mr. Pen. "Now, Marc, I have one more question for you. Do you think this man needs art?"

Marc laughed. "Are you going to give him this picture? He would sell it as soon as he could. You know that!"

"Go deeper, Marc," said Mr. Pen. "I didn't ask if he needed this picture. I asked if he needed art."

Art? What did that mean? Marc thought

about everything he and Mr. Pen had talked about. He thought about the pictures he had drawn. He thought of all the things he loved that no one else ever seemed to notice. The clouds in the sky. A calf behind a fence. Two old men playing a game of chess. His father rolling a barrel of herring down the street.

"Yes," Marc said at last. "He needs art. We all need art to show us what is truly beautiful and important in the world. We need art to show us the small, secret things that we never take time to see. We need art to show us how to live, how to be alive in the world. Otherwise, we will become like Baron Karpf and his family, always looking into the magic mirror and seeing nothing but ourselves."

"That's exactly how I feel," said Mr. Pen. "There is more to art than making pretty pictures. What is beautiful is not always true.

But what is true is always beautiful, in its own way. That is what artists do. They seek out what is true and show it to the world."

He held out his hand to Marc. "Now you know what an artist does. Do you think you'd like to become one? Lessons only cost five rubles a month. You can start this week."

"I'll have to talk to my parents," Marc said. "My father works in a herring warehouse. We don't have a lot of money."

Mr. Pen shrugged. "Those are the students who do best, the ones who have to struggle. Talk to your parents, but no matter what they say, come see me again. If you truly want to be an artist, there is always a way. We will find it together."

Marc shook hands with Mr. Pen. "Thank you, sir. You have given me a great gift today." He hurried down the stairs and into the street. His whole body felt light, as if he were flying over the rooftops, like the boy in his drawing.

Marc was halfway home when he remembered that he had not shown Mr. Pen any of his drawings. Nor had Mr. Pen asked to see them.

I will show them to him later, when I come back, Marc thought.

6

Pitchkas!

Marc ran all the way home. "I am going to be an artist," he said to himself over and over again. He burst through the door. He saw his mother standing by the stove. She had spent the day making bread. Flour covered her arms to the elbows. She put the loaves on a long-handled baker's shovel and, bending low, carefully placed them in the oven.

Marc pulled the shovel from her hands. Gripping her by the elbows, he danced her around the kitchen.

"What's the matter with you, Marc?" his mother cried. "Have you gone crazy?"

"I am crazy, Mother. Forgive me. I can't help it. Something wonderful happened to me today," Marc said. "My whole life opened up like a book. I know what I want to be."

"What?" his mother asked.

Marc opened his arms wide. He shouted loud enough for everyone on Pokrovskaya Street to hear. "An artist! I'm going to be an artist!"

Marc's mother brushed the flour from her apron. She looked at Marc as if he really had gone crazy. "What are you talking about? Have you lost your wits? What in the world is an artist?"

"An artist makes pictures, Mother," Marc explained.

"Pitchkas? What do you mean?" Marc's mother could not understand him.

"I'll show you," Marc said. He opened the envelope that held his drawings. One by one, he stuck them on the walls, just as he had seen in Mr. Pen's studio. Someday, when he was a famous artist, he would cover the walls of his own studio with pictures. For now, his mother's kitchen would have to do.

Marc's mother put the last of the loaves in the oven. She walked around the kitchen, staring at Marc's drawings. "What is this?" she asked him.

"This is art," said Marc.

Marc's mother wrinkled her nose. "This is craziness. What do I see here? A cat. A fish. A horse. A rooster. So? How is this going to feed a family?" She pointed to the picture of Grandfather's house. "Why is Uncle Noah on the roof? When did you ever see him climbing around on the roof with a fiddle?"

Marc wanted to crawl into the oven with the loaves. He had felt so happy only moments before. Now he felt worse than when he brought home a bad report card.

But he wasn't ready to give up. Marc tried to explain what artists do, the way Mr. Pen had explained it to him. Marc's mother could not understand. "Pitchkas show me how to see? Do I need eyeglasses? If I want to see horses and chickens, I'll go out in the street. There are plenty of them there. And God forbid I should ever see a fiddler dancing around on the roof! I'd let out such a yell it would break the windowpanes."

At this moment, the door opened and Marc's father walked in. His clothes were damp and streaked with salt. He smelled of fish.

"Why are you shouting? Who fell off the roof?" Marc's father asked.

"Nobody fell off the roof, Haskel," Marc's mother said. "Marc has been drawing pitchkas. He wants to be an artist."

"Pitchkas?" Marc's father wrinkled his brow. "Oh, you mean *pictures*. I've seen lots of pictures. They're in the newspaper at work that we use to wrap the herring." His fingers twisted the strands of his beard. He turned to the pictures pinned to the walls.

His eyes opened wide as he stopped before Marc's drawings.

"Did you make these?" he asked Marc.

"Yes, Papa," Marc said with pride. "My friend Victor says they are very good."

"I don't care what Victor says," said Mr. Chagall. "He's only a boy. What does he know about anything? All I see is nonsense. Is this how you waste your time when you should be studying your lessons?"

"These are good, Papa!" Marc's sister Manya declared. The commotion had brought the girls to the kitchen. They gathered around Marc's pictures. They laughed and pointed when they saw people or animals they knew. "Marc can draw!" they all agreed.

"Be still. Nobody's talking to you," Marc's father snapped at the girls.

"Papa's right," his mother said. "Who

cares if Marc can draw or not? Better he should study and learn."

Marc felt himself shrinking toward the floor. His parents' scolding made him feel as tiny as a mouse. But a mouse, at least, could run away and hide in a mouse hole. There was no running away for Marc. He had to stand and listen without saying a word as his father, then his mother, told him how lazy he was.

"We spend a fortune sending you to school so you can have a future. Is this how you repay us?" Marc's father was shouting now, waving his arms as he stamped back and forth across the kitchen. "You're throwing your life away! You're wasting time making pictures instead of studying books!" He was so angry his voice shook.

"You don't know how lucky you are," Marc's mother added. "You can go to school. Nobody else in our family ever had that chance. Someone needs to teach you a lesson."

Marc's father turned to his mother. "I'm going to give him that lesson. Tomorrow morning I'm taking Marc to work with me. Let him spend a day in the herring factory. He'll see how hard it is to work for a living. Maybe that will inspire him to change his ways."

Marc's mother grasped him by the chin. She lifted his head so he was staring into her eyes. "Papa means business. So do I! This is your last chance, Marc. Take a good look at the herring factory. If you don't start studying harder, that's going to be your future."

Red-faced and trembling, Marc left the kitchen. He tried hard not to cry. His whole life had fallen apart. His dream of becoming an artist had disappeared into the cracks of the kitchen floor. He would be lucky if his parents even allowed him to continue going to school. Most likely, he would end up working beside his father in the herring factory. For the rest of his life!

"Here, Marc. Wc saved these for you." His sisters handed him the pictures he had stuck on the kitchen wall.

"We were afraid Mama and Papa would tear them up and throw them into the stove," said Manya. "They're really angry."

"I know," said Marc as he took his precious bundle of drawings. "They'll never let me draw another picture again. I'll never be an artist."

"Oh, yes you will!" said Manya. "You'll find a way."

7

The Herring Artist

*T*hat night Marc had a dream. He dreamed that he stood at the easel in Mr. Pen's studio, painting a picture of a man wearing the apron and leather cap his father wore to work at the herring factory. But the man that Marc painted wasn't his father. It wasn't a man at all! It was an enormous herring wearing his father's clothes. The herring stared at him with goggly fish eyes. It spoke to him.

"Hurry up, Marc! We have to get to work."

Marc sat up in bed. He stared into his dark room. What a strange dream! The easel and the herring were gone, but the apron and leather cap were very much still there. Marc's father was dressed for work, even though the sun had yet to come up. It was time for Marc to join him.

"Do you think you're going to sleep all day? Let's go! The boss is waiting." Marc's father pulled the feather quilt off the bed. The cold air stung Marc's skin like a swarm of bees. "That will get you moving!" his father said. "Get dressed. I'll meet you in the kitchen."

Marc rubbed his eyes. The big herring hadn't been a pleasant subject, but at least he'd enjoyed creating a picture. Marc wondered if he would ever have the chance to do that again. Maybe only in his dreams.

He buttoned on a flannel shirt, an old sweater with worn-out elbows, and a much-patched pair of trousers. He pulled thick woolen socks over his feet and a pair of tall boots over them. Marc wouldn't be wearing his handsome school uniform today. Work at the herring factory was cold, wet, and dirty.

Marc hurried to the kitchen. His mother was already up and making breakfast. She cut thick slabs of black bread and put them on the table, along with a plate of pickled herring and two steaming glasses of hot tea.

"You'd better eat, Marc," his mother said. "You're going to need all your strength to get through the day."

"Mama's right," his father said. "You're going to be wishing you were in that nice, warm schoolroom pushing a pencil around."

Why can't I make them understand?

Marc thought as he picked at his breakfast. *I don't want to be in the herring factory. I don't want to be in the classroom. All I want to do is make pictures.*

"Here's something to take with you. I don't want you to be hungry," said Marc's mother as she handed him his lunch of black bread and herring wrapped in newspaper.

"Thank you, Mama," said Marc.

"We're not doing this to punish you," his father said. "It's to teach you an important lesson. One day you'll thank me for it."

"I know, Papa," said Marc, although he didn't feel thankful at all.

Marc and his father started down the street toward the herring factory. By the time they got there, the cold winter sun had just begun to peep up over the edge of the river.

The herring factory squatted on the banks of the river, smelling of fish, mud, and salt.

The tumbledown building built of weather-beaten boards made Marc think of Noah's ark. It seemed to be as ancient. A blanket of green moss covered the roof. White stains left by perching seagulls and pigeons streaked the sides.

Marc followed his father down a rickety
ramp that led to a dock beside the river.
Marc saw a barge loaded with barrels tied up
alongside a large wooden crane. Two bear-
like figures in leather aprons stood beside
the crane, looking down into the barge.

"Vanya! Jasek!" Marc's father called.

The two bears looked up and waved back. "Hello, Haskel! Who's that dwarf with you?"

"This is my boy Marc. He came to work here for a day to see what it's like," Marc's father said.

The two bears laughed. "We can show him that, all right!"

As Marc came closer, he saw that the two bears were enormous men. They towered over his father. Vanya had a long beard that came down to his waist. He had long, curly black hair and wore a black sheepskin cap. Marc could hardly tell where the hair ended and the sheepskin began.

Jasek, Vanya's partner, had a huge mustache. The ends of the mustache hung down so far below his chin that he could have braided them together. Marc wished he had some paper and a pencil. He would have liked to draw them.

Vanya and Jasek shook hands with Marc. Their great paws swallowed his tiny hand. Marc felt scared at first, but only for a moment. He soon saw that Vanya and Jasek, as big and strong as they were, were gentle, friendly fellows.

"I want Marc to stay with you this morning," Marc's father said. "He needs to learn what it's like to work really hard. Nobody here works harder than you two."

"We can teach him that, all right," Jasek and Vanya said. "Don't worry, Marc. The work may be hard at first, but you'll get used to it. We were no bigger than you when we started." They both laughed long and hard, sharing a joke that Marc didn't think was one bit funny.

Vanya jumped onto the barge. Jasek

walked Marc around to the back of the crane. The icy wind blowing across the river made Marc shiver. His fingers ached from the cold. He put them in his pockets to warm them while Jasek explained what they had to do.

"The herring come from up north, from the Baltic Sea. They're gutted, salted, and packed into barrels. The barrels are loaded onto barges and brought upriver to towns like Vitebsk. We store the herring here in the factory and sell them to the people in town. Some we leave salted. We pickle the rest in brine. You can do a lot with herring. That's why people in Vitebsk love to eat it. It's cheap and it's good. Black bread, herring, and a slice of onion. What could be better! The tsar himself never ate anything so delicious!"

The tsar ruled all of Russia from his

capital in St. Petersburg. Marc had seen many pictures of him and his family in the magazine he borrowed from the library. Marc imagined the tsar, sitting on his throne in his crown and royal robes, eating herring, black bread, and onions from a gold plate. The idea made him laugh. *That* was a picture he would like to draw!

Jasek lined up the ropes of the crane. "Here's what we'll do now," he told Marc. "We unload the barrels from the barge. Vanya will lash a rope around the barrel and hook it up to the crane. We pull it up and lower it to the dock. Then we roll it up the ramp into the factory, to the place where it will be stored."

"Tell me what to do," said Marc. The work didn't strike him as hard.

"Take hold of the rope," said Jasek. "When Vanya gives the signal, pull as hard as you can until the barrel comes up from the barge. I'll swing the crane around. You lower the barrel to the dock. Do it slowly. These barrels can break open if they're dropped too hard. Then we have a mess of herring all over the place and the boss gets mad. You don't want to have Mr. Klepfish mad at you. No, sir!"

"Ready! Hoist 'er up!" Vanya called from the barge. He'd lashed a rope around the first barrel and hooked the crane to it.

"Pull, Marc!" said Jasek.

Marc pulled. Nothing happened. The barrel did not budge.

"You have to pull hard," said Vanya.

"I *am* pulling hard!" Marc replied. He wrapped the rope around his hands, leaned his shoulder against it, and pulled, pulled, pulled.

The barrel did not budge.

"I'm sorry," said Marc. His frozen hands were red and sore from pulling on the rope. His shoulders ached. The cold wind blew more fiercely than before. Bits of sleet stung his face. He wished he were back in school. Even the dullest history lesson was better than this.

Jasek didn't seem to mind the cold or the wind. "It's not your fault," he said. "You're just a boy and this is a heavy barrel. It's as big as you are. I'll bet it weighs more."

"What are we going to do?" Vanya asked. "These barrels aren't going to get any lighter."

"Marc needs help," Jasek decided. He came around to the back of the crane and took hold of the rope. "Okay, Marc. I'll pull, and you'll pull with me. Ready? Here we go. Pull!"

Jasek and Marc pulled together. Marc

tugged and strained. The heavy barrel rose slowly out of the barge. "We did it!" said Marc.

"Now I'm going around to turn the crane," Jasek said. "You hold on to the rope. Don't let the barrel drop."

"I won't!" said Marc. He held on to the rope as tightly as he could. But as soon as Jasek let go of the rope, the barrel dropped back down onto the barge. Marc, holding tight to the rope, felt himself yanked high into the air.

"Help!" he shouted. But the wind blew so loudly that nobody heard him.

The barrel landed with a thump, shaking the whole barge. It bobbed up and down in the river like a cork.

"Somebody help me! Please!" Marc called again.

Jasek and Vanya looked up. They began

to laugh. "Marc looks like a fish on a line. Let go!" they said. Marc let go of the rope. He dropped to the dock.

This was turning into the worst day of Marc's life, and it was far from over. Nothing he did was right. Jasek and Vanya meant to be kind. He couldn't blame them for laughing at him. Marc felt like a dunce. He was cold, damp, and miserable.

"This isn't going to work," he said. He was glad the wind made his face red so Jasek and Vanya couldn't see how embarrassed he was.

"You're right," Jasek and Vanya agreed. "But it's not your fault. These barrels are heavy. You want to work, but you're not strong enough. We'll have to find another way for you to help."

"What else can I do?" Marc asked.

"I know!" said Vanya. "Your father says

you go to school. Can you read and write?"

"Of course," said Marc.

"Well, we can't," Jasek told him. "We never went to school. Are you good with numbers?"

"Yes," Marc answered.

"Then I know how you can help us," Jasek said. "We can handle the barrels. What we can't handle are the numbers. We're always getting the count wrong. Then the boss gets mad."

"We'll unload the barge. You keep track of the barrels," Vanya added.

Marc, Vanya, and Jasek worked until the barge was unloaded. Vanya and Jasek moved the barrels. Marc sat cross-legged on the dock with a ledger book balanced on his knees. A pencil was tied to the ledger with a string so it wouldn't get lost.

Marc read the writing on the top of each

barrel. He noted where it came from, the kind and number of herring it held, whether they'd end up salted or pickled. He entered all the information in the ledger, along with where in the factory the barrel was to be stored.

However, there wasn't a lot for Marc to do while Vanya and Jasek lashed, hauled, and rolled barrels. Marc enjoyed watching them. The two big men worked as a team. They moved as gracefully as dancers. *I wish I could draw them,* Marc thought. *Why not? I have plenty of time, and there's plenty of paper in this ledger book.*

Marc opened the ledger book to the last page. He took the pencil and began to draw. He drew Jasek hauling a barrel up from the barge. He drew Vanya bending over, lashing a rope around the barrel. He drew both men rolling barrels up the ramp into the factory.

Then his imagination took hold. He drew Vanya as a dog with a long board and Jasek, with his long mustache, as a cat. Herring flew through the air. They hovered over the barge like a flock of birds. Marc drew his father sitting cross-legged on the roof of the factory, playing the fiddle while the Vanya dog and the Jasek cat danced in a circle with the herring.

"What is this? What are you doing with my ledger?"

Marc slammed the ledger shut. The pencil came loose and rolled across the dock. Marc grabbed for it, looking up at the same time. A tall, thin man in a black fur coat with a hat to match and a pointed yellow beard stared down at him. "Who are you?" the man asked.

"That's Haskel's son, Boss!" Jasek yelled from the barge. "He came in to work today."

"He's too little to haul barrels," Vanya added. "But he can read and write. We put him to work keeping the ledger."

"Maybe it will come out right this time," the man grumbled. He turned to Marc. "What I saw didn't look like numbers. I'll ask you again. What were you doing?"

Marc knew who the man was. It was Mr. Klepfish, the owner of the factory. Why had he been so foolish? What could he have been thinking of to draw pictures in an important book like the factory ledger? Mr. Klepfish was going to be furious. Marc's father might lose his job. If that happened, what would become of their family?

Marc's voice trembled as he answered. "I'm sorry, sir. I was drawing pictures."

"Pictures, eh?" said Mr. Klepfish. "Let me see them."

Marc handed him the ledger. Mr. Klepfish

turned the pages, looking at Marc's drawings. He smiled when he came to the one of the herring dancing with the dog and the cat.

"I like these," he said. He handed the ledger back to Marc. "You've made this loading dock more interesting than it usually is. I talked with your father when I came to work today. He tells me you want to be an artist. Good for you! I had dreams myself once. Hold on to yours. Don't let them get away."

He reached into his pocket, took something out, and pressed it into Marc's hand. Marc stared. It was a ten-ruble silver coin.

"I suppose these drawings belong to me, since they're in my ledger," Mr. Klepfish said. "Still, I want to be fair. Consider this your first sale as an artist." He gave Marc a wink. "Whatever you do, don't give up your dreams. Don't get caught in the herring factory."

Marc was so surprised he hardly knew what to say. "I won't!" he promised, although he had no idea how he would keep that promise.

"Can you believe it?" Marc's father told his mother that evening when they returned home. "The boss gave Marc ten rubles for some pictures he drew in the back of the ledger."

"Ten rubles? That's as much as you earn in a day, Haskel!" Marc's mother exclaimed.

"Maybe we've been too hasty," Marc's father continued. "Mr. Klepfish came by to have a talk with me. He said Marc had talent and if he wanted to become an artist, we should let him."

"Mr. Klepfish always knows what he's talking about," Marc's mother agreed. "Maybe we should think more about this. Perhaps we should talk with that teacher, Mr. Pen."

"You're lucky," Marc's sister Manya whispered to him as they listened to their parents talking at the kitchen table.

"Do you really think they'll let me become an artist?" Marc asked her.

"Of course!" Manya said. "Yesterday they laughed at the idea. Now they're talking about it. Give them time. It will happen. You're almost there. I wish I were as lucky as you."

Manya's words forced Marc to think. *I am lucky,* he thought. Manya never had the chance to go to school. It didn't matter what she wanted to be. She was a girl, and girls had only one future. They became wives and mothers. They cooked, cleaned, and raised children, as their mothers and grandmothers did.

"You have dreams. You should have a chance, too," said Marc.

Manya shrugged her shoulders. "Maybe I will someday," she said. "But there is one thing you can do for me now. Show me what Mr. Pen teaches you. I think I'd like to learn about art. Maybe someday you'll paint a pitchka of me!"

"I will," Marc promised.

8

Over Vitebsk

Marc walked to Mr. Pen's house after dinner. He knocked on the door. Mr. Pen opened it.

"Hello, Mr. Pen," Marc said. "I hope I'm not bothering you. I talked with my parents. They're going to let me study with you."

Mr. Pen shook Marc's hand. "Congratulations! Please come in, Marc. You're not bothering me at all. We have a lot to talk about. Would you like some tea?"

"Yes, please," Marc said. He sat down at the table, clutching the envelope that held his drawings. He had brought them for Mr. Pen to see.

A shining brass samovar sat in the middle of the table with a small teapot on top. Charcoal in the samovar heated the water and kept the tea warm. Mr. Pen prepared a glass of tea for Marc in the Russian way. He filled the glass half full with strong black tea. He added hot water from the samovar until the glass was full.

"Would you like sugar or jam?" Mr. Pen asked. Some people in Russia used jam to sweeten their tea. Other people held a sugar cube in their mouth while they drank it.

"No, thank you," said Marc.

Mr. Pen looked through the envelope as

Marc sipped his tea. Marc couldn't help feeling nervous as Mr. Pen spread his drawings out on the table, studying them one by one. This was the first time Marc had shown Mr. Pen his work. What would he think of the drawings? Were they any good? Would he like them, or would he think they were strange?

Marc waited for Mr. Pen to say something, but the minutes went without him or Marc saying anything at all. Marc swallowed the last of his tea.

"These are interesting," Mr. Pen finally said. "Most of my students begin by drawing objects or people. You've drawn some amusing scenes. Why is that fiddler on the roof?"

"I don't know," Marc replied. "It seemed right at the time. Is it wrong?"

"Not at all," said Mr. Pen. "There is no right or wrong in art. The artist alone decides. People may like the work or they may not. They may think the artist is crazy. But that does not make it wrong. If you want your fiddler on the roof, that's where he belongs."

Mr. Pen collected Marc's pictures and put them back in the envelope. He pinned a piece of paper to a drawing board and placed it in front of Marc. Next to it he placed a tray filled with pencils and sticks of artist's charcoal.

"I'd like you to draw something for me, Marc," Mr. Pen said.

Marc picked a pencil from the tray. "What should I draw?" he asked.

"Remember what I told you," Mr. Pen answered. "You're the artist. Draw whatever pleases you. Draw anything you like." Mr. Pen carried the tea glasses and the samovar into the kitchen, leaving Marc alone in the room. "Take as much time as you need. Call me when you're done," he said.

Marc took a pencil in his hand. He stared at the blank paper. What should he draw? Marc's mind went blank. He couldn't think of anything.

Marc scribbled aimlessly on the corner of the paper. He looked out the window. *Maybe I can find an idea out there,* he thought.

A bright moon hung in the sky over

Vitebsk, lighting up the street and the rooftops. Before he was even aware of it, Marc's fingers began to move. The pencil traced lines across the paper. Marc looked down at the paper and smiled. He knew what he wanted to draw now.

Vitebsk began to appear on the paper. Here was Marc's house, with his mother and sisters hanging out laundry in the backyard. There was the herring factory. Vanya and Jasek stood aboard a barge, unloading barrels of herring. Here was the market and the town hall, a nobleman riding in a carriage, a priest leading a religious procession, a policeman standing on a street corner, two soldiers coming out of a tavern, their arms around each other's shoulders as they reeled down the street. All the sights, sounds, and smells of Vitebsk went into Marc's picture. His pencil danced across the paper.

"I'm finished," he called out at last.

Mr. Pen came back into the room. "I'm eager to see what you've drawn," he said. He picked up a pencil as he examined Marc's picture. The clock on the wall ticked by the minutes. Every now and then, Mr. Pen drew some lines on the paper. He straightened an arm, the roof of a house. Marc saw how Mr. Pen's changes improved his drawings. Mr. Pen was a very good teacher, Marc decided. He could learn a lot from him.

At last, Mr. Pen looked up. He turned to Marc. "Not bad. Actually, this drawing is rather good for someone who has taught himself. You do have a lot to learn. But that's for later. I like this picture very much, except . . ."

"Is something wrong with it?" Marc asked.

"Ah, remember what I said. Nothing in art is wrong. However, I feel that something important is missing," said Mr. Pen. "All of Vitebsk is here. Horses, soldiers, chickens. But not Marc. Where are you? Where is Marc in this picture?"

Marc looked at his picture again. He never thought of putting himself in it. Yet wasn't that what Mr. Pen had talked about before? The picture belongs to the artist. That must mean that the artist always puts himself in the picture in some way. His thoughts, his feelings—perhaps even the artist himself—become part of it.

"Now I understand," Marc whispered to himself. He knew exactly what to do. In the space between the moon and the stars, above the steeples and rooftops of Vitebsk, he drew a boy with wings. A boy like himself, flying high in the sky over Vitebsk.

"Who is he, this flying boy?" Mr. Pen asked when Marc finished.

"It's me," said Marc. "The wings are my dreams. They've carried me higher than I could ever imagine. Beyond school. Beyond the herring factory. Maybe, someday, even beyond Vitebsk. Do you think that can happen, Mr. Pen?"

"Anything can happen, Marc," Mr. Pen said. "The future belongs to you, like your picture. It becomes what you, the artist, put into it." He pinned a fresh piece of paper to the drawing board. "Shall we have our first lesson?"

"I'm ready," said Marc, picking up the pencil. "Let's begin."

Author's Note

A *Picture for Marc* is based on actual events in the life of Marc Chagall (1887–1985), one of the twentieth century's greatest artists.

Yehuda Pen (1854–1937) played an important role as a teacher of artists, although he was not a noteworthy artist himself. Since many of his students could not afford to pay tuition, Pen allowed them to study and paint in his studio for free. His little school in Vitebsk provided the only opportunity for students like Marc Chagall to acquire an artistic education. El Lissitzky, another prominent Russian Jewish artist, was also one of Pen's students.

Although I use the name Marc in this story, Chagall didn't call himself that until years later. His childhood name was Moishe (Moses). The family's name was originally Segal, pronounced "Shegal" in the dialect of the region. Marc's father adopted the name Shagal, which means "to take big steps" in Russian. Marc was greatly influenced by French painters and ultimately settled in France. *Chagall* is the French spelling of *Shagal*.

Readers wishing to learn more about Marc Chagall and his times will find valuable information in the following books:

Alexander, Sidney. *Marc Chagall: A Biography*. New York: Putnam, 1978.

Bohm-Duchen, Monica. *Chagall*. London: Phaidon Press, 1998.

Chagall, Marc. *My Life*. London: Peter Owen Publishers, 2003.

Crespelle, Jean-Paul. *The Love, the Dreams, the Life of Chagall*. Trans. Benita Eisler. New York: Coward-McCann, 1970.

Harshav, Benjamin. *Marc Chagall and His Times: A Documentary Narrative*. Stanford, Calif.: Stanford University Press, 2004.

About the Author

Eric A. Kimmel grew up in Brooklyn, New York. He is the award-winning author of several well-known children's books, including *Anansi and the Moss-Covered Rock* and the Caldecott Honor Book *Hershel and the Hanukkah Goblins,* as well as another Stepping Stone book, *A Horn for Louis.* He and his wife, Doris, live in Portland, Oregon.

About the Illustrator

Matthew Trueman grew up in Italy forty-five minutes north of Venice. He still lives by the water, now the Delaware River, with his wife, Anna, and their cat, Fisher. His luminous artwork can be seen in *Noah's Mittens* and *When the Chickens Went on Strike*, which was a 2003 Sydney Taylor Honor Book for Younger Readers.

If you liked *A Picture for Marc,*
read Eric A. Kimmel's

A Horn for Louis

Louis saw guitars, trombones, and clarinets hanging in the window. He saw saxophones, violins, and banjos. And one trumpet!

The trumpet looked new. Its polished brass shined. Louis stood on tiptoe. He pressed his nose against the window. The trumpet was the most beautiful horn Louis had ever seen. Then he looked at the price tag.

Twenty-five dollars!

Louis's shoulders sagged. He looked at the silver dollar in his hand. That trumpet might as well have been made of gold.